By Reason of Breakings

By Reason of Breakings

Poems by Andrew Zawacki

THE UNIVERSITY OF GEORGIA PRESS

ATHENS AND LONDON

Published by the University of Georgia Press

Athens, Georgia 30602

© 2002 by Andrew Zawacki

Designed by Betty Palmer McDaniel

Set in 10.5/13 Walbaum

Printed and bound by McNaughton & Gunn

The paper in this book meets the guidelines for

permanence and durability of the Committee on

Production Guidelines for Book Longevity of the

Council on Library Resources.

Printed in the United States of America

06 05 04 03 02 P 5 4 3 2 1

Library of Congress Cataloging-in-Publication Data

Zawacki, Andrew, 1972–

By reason of breakings : poems / by Andrew Zawacki.

p. cm.

ISBN 0-8203-2341-1 (alk. paper)

I. Title

PS3626.A93 B9 2002

811'.6—dc21   2001037626

British Library Cataloging-in-Publication Data available

for J

Contents

Part Three

§

Acknowledgments

Grateful acknowledgments are due to the editors of the following publications, in which many of the poems, occasionally in different form, have appeared: *The Age, Agni, American Letters & Commentary, The Antioch Review, The Australian, Black Warrior Review, Boston Review, Connecticut Poetry Review, Denver Quarterly, Fence, Gulf Coast, Hayden's Ferry Review, The Literary Review, Meanjin, Metre, New American Writing, The New Republic, Nova revija, nowCulture, The Oxford Quarterly, Ploughshares, Poetry Ireland Review, Poetryetc., The Prose Poem: An International Journal, Quarterly West, Salt, Semtext / Plastic, Slope, Southerly, Southern Humanities Review, Southwest Review, Verse, Volt, The William and Mary Review*, and *The Yale Review*.

A version of "Note from Anotherwhere" first appeared in the annual Vilenica chapbook (Društvo slovenskih pisateljev, 1997). "Ampersonata" first appeared in *Voices for Kosovo*, edited by Rupert Loydell (Stride, 1999). Parts of *"Mise en scène"* appeared in *The Best of "The Prose Poem: An International Journal,"* edited by Peter Johnson (White Pine Press, 2000), and in *Catalyst*, edited by John Kinsella (Salt/Folio, 2001).

Thank you to these institutions, for their generous assistance: The Rhodes Scholarship Trust, Slovenian Writers' Association, Hawthornden Castle International Retreat for Writers, Millay Colony for the Arts, Constance Saltonstall Foundation for the Arts, and the Pennsylvania Council on the Arts.

Many thanks also to Lois Conaway, Bill Coyle, Robert Crawford, Joanne Dearcopp, Aleš Debeljak, Timothy Donnelly, Douglas Dunn, Forrest Gander, Henry Hart, Lukas Haynes, Michael Heller, Ernie Hilbert, Christine Hume, Jane Kotapish, Timothy Liu, Bin Ramke, Tomaž Šalamun, Mark Strand, Cam Walker, and Charles Wright. Thank you to my parents John and Cathryn, especially my mother, who played travel agent for each of these poems. And thanks foremost to Brian Henry, who ushered this book *from spark to phoenish.*

yet not so broken and cut off from

ST. AUGUSTINE

Vespers

Architecture it's not, not even in winter.
Nor is it a draft of a river
to be put away for a lover to polish up later
after the nails have been paid. Nor
is it the finished thing
even if it has the look of a finished thing. In winter
but it is not winter, it's almost a year ago. Water
that's moving cannot be called a trigger
but almost a need. Our bodies are not architecture,
they're moving, they have been put away by October.
A draft of an almost finished river
is not a crowblue cloud at the end of winter, but after
accounts have been paid, years later, a whisper
is polished up to have the look of architecture.
October has the look of a crow in a river. It's a year
ago, our bodies are four-fifths water. Your
body is polished up to have the look of moving water.
Clouds are four-fifths of winter, but whatever
is almost crowblue or moving cannot be called architecture
or put away for our bodies to polish up later.
I did not say nails had been put away, or paid for
with our bodies' whispered accounts. I did not say fever
or finished, or after; I did not call winter a need. I never
said I had been nailed to a river
even if you had the look of what's already left.

Part One

Astrelegy

Light in the shipyards is so long in coming
the stars it once belonged to aren't there any more.

Zodiac bends in formaldehyde, where the turnpike
crosses two rivers shimmying north: Gemini

making love for the last time, zero degrees in collapse.
The twins already know about order and arc,

having learned the lesson of giving up
to lay themselves down by springrusted locks

in the bridge; backwater silt records their horoscope,
folded each night and beginning to fray at the edge:

The moon, it's written, *keeps taking the sea
from the sea, and giving it back to the sea.*

Death is not for the dying:
stars above the boathouse are playing

Cyrano to light, which remembers their names
but forgets the whiteiron scars:

this leftover light is a handful of dirt
to what finished before you were born,

and even when stars come unstuck and fall through,
it tricks us, too, into mourning.

Wherefrom the Shadows that Are Forms

Escorting the immediate ornament of dream
    it lingered past the absence it invoked
like a thunderstorm, decisive in its indifference,
    that over a folded, unfamiliar premise
recast the decadent frieze allure had let go:
    sharpening of caution along a branch,
expansion into dark, elaborate fields
    where, because it had not yet inquired,
trees resisted wind that sounded of nothing,
    no place, nobody known,
already other than why it was setting out:
    closing in of clouds, forgotten forms,
dusk erotic blue at the river's inflection
    as if, by encountering its design,
an end was reached before the terms were met:
    across the outer suspicions of grass
teased by a wrapped, a razor moon
    heavier for its weight against a hill,
it stayed above an interior lit from within
    at the edge of sight: where we,
because we lived there, were never at home.

Ventriloquy

Not nails but the hammer,
having been there before and vanished,
is the house.

As bones consumed by fire
become the fire.

As a boy is a god since his face
is the face of a trickster,
and a puppet is neither himself nor another.

Since voice is an echo
already too late.

Not bones but the voice that says
Be thou bone
is the flint.

That the voice is the voice of a god
and vanished through doors.

As nails are consumed by a hammer
and a puppet who burns a house
becomes the flint and then the fire.

As an echo,
having been there before,
is consumed.

That a voice saying *Be thou bone*
is not a door,

as the face of a boy
is neither himself nor another.

Since a god,
having been there before,
is already too late.

Since the house is a trickster's house
and the bones are yours.

Slipknot 1

By which I mean the saboteur is among us

By which I mean a needle

A doll, the lateness of dolls

By which I mean updraft in each of the corners

By which I mean to say boxcar

A pipistrelle

A coin, a comma

By which is meant vicinity

By which I mean apropos, I mean position

I mean asymptote

By which I mean a bystander

A lullaby, a proctor's kiss

By heir and error

By reason of breakings

By which I mean they've gone by now

The island I mean, mean stature, mean stone

By which I mean mistaking midwinter for glass

By which I mean a hurrying home, or homeward

A laceration, not spiral not curve

A window, a feverfew scent

By which I mean unproven

By which is meant anatomy

A leaf, an asking

A leaf

Note from Anotherwhere

Too much peace, someone told us,
can break a man apart

yet we could not stop moving in front
of that phrase or what it might have meant

had we not been the ones who heard it first,
sandhi rippling with every stroke of light

into the morning: sometimes we'd turn
our clocks ahead in autumn

or unwind them an hour in spring
as a mother might arrive at a house to find

the door has already been opened,
whoever was inside gone out.

There is little give and take
walking backward into winter:

half-parsed wind through sumac and birch
has never been seen in this town

where a letter from across the street
is an answer, and sometimes isn't

for those who live and die by what
the mailbox brings, and doesn't.

Self-Portrait

Only the colorless eye is undistracted: a lake
rubbed blue by twilight is not blue to the eye cast blue
and a violet sunset cannot be refracted
violet through the violet eye. A crimson retina
won't conceive the paint of a rigging blooded by dusk
or the stain a star makes, cutting its patina
crimson across a backwind disturbing the houseboat.

An idol requiring concealment, the eye is hewn
without discernible hue, conferring the spectrum it lacks:
eviscerated axiom of presence, the eye is a naught
diffracting weather and water, and exits itself for the sake
of what it reveals: a condition of vantage, a contract
with the mooring ropes and canvas it perceives,
cataract the extracted vanishing point.

The pupil is polished black as the hull of a yacht
so the eye won't recognize darkness, only the fact
of its coming on: a knot of isinglass that reflects
lightning tracing paraphs around the harbor, it receives
faint shadows enshrouding the dock, and orders by its law.
Not as judge but witness, emptying act for clarity
yet inverting marina and watchman, as if to deceive:

surface uncracked, improved upon, the eye is nothing it saw.

Any Other Eviction, Than the Frequent

If it be warfare, let it be mistress
and midnight up that slope,
not reticent in a weather
of withdrawal, its salmon-roe tint,
the shabby grass it grazes

but varnished to richterline
under a prismatic glare:
delinquent churn of cloudswath
and gust, calving a foreshore filth
from its respiratory lunge:

inlaid verges blear kaleidoscopic,
larkspur and loosestrife splinter
and render afire, as frontiers to scour
or confiscate, and laving dark
these latent, these restive affronts:

I was in love with a river
and its recoil—water and whither
it went is a doctrine of veil,
appliqué to what angle of incident
little, what lightless, unhinge.

Argument for an Elemental Aesthetic

—deficiency implies
local forecast & fruition
& the climate of a country
without which it wavers:

discretion & exposure,
say, or uncompromising
intimacy of snow

—at a prospect of spruce
wrapped in burlap & twine
these are perhaps
authentic intelligences:

propane & pressed
metal, glass-
blowing, tool-&-die

or mind to which a body
owes advent & end

—consider creekthaw & say-
brook floe, nonchalance
of shipman's eddy
laminated in ice,

sandstone ritz
scattered with salt,
low watermark of a rise:

such unconstrained gestures
of central speed, at once
centripetal, insecure,

are contours
propelled by interiors
otherwise unimposed

—not derrick
but diesel & disarray,
runaway ramp
when brakes refuse braking

are limits assumed
as instance of incompletion
not its cause:

aria blurred
to a claywash crease,
bootjack hill glisted sere,

clouds disguised
by ground that does not guess
or let them go

Slipknot 2

A cloud that comes between is not a cloud

A lung is not circle or line

Color does not recur

An engine is not nomenclature

Nor does a letter relinquish its splint

A border is not and desisting is not

Nor is a bridge its projection or purpose

A nerve is not unwrapped if ushered open

To alter is not to accept or acquire

Vocative is not symbol not valve

Neither presumed nor imposed

A tremor is not lever or latch

Not requisite design

Valence not after vacancy after vox

A shadow is not fermata not form

Nor movement toward or away

The Hour between Midnight and Midnight

Was it the radical insufficiency, the snow in the rooms and walking
from one to the other? Was it the iced-over pantomime of sleeping

under a false set of stars, interrogating angels and getting nowhere?
Was it how, in the imperfect wind-ordered arch of a neighbor's lake,

the moonlit yard became a palindrome, a symmetry too still to allow us
to enter, dancing as we were, away from our private lives? Was it

an unintended isomer, or cloud cover to an intimacy colored just beyond
the view our window afforded? Was it coming down the stairs unseen

and was there no way to stop it from stopping, to slow its intricate slowing,
or was it what we thought we heard, calling to us from below the arc lights

with us pretending to miss it? What else could it have been if not the hour
between midnight and midnight, a meridian of suspended acoustics and torque,

when you turned to me and, living it over, said these were the orchestrations
of two glaciers fretting, but it would take more than that to see in the dark.

Slipknot 3

If unrecovered or fashioned as rigor

If into and out of a center

If the visitor once received should depart

To improvise or improve

Across the water's charade across foyer

If seraglio if sign

If conviction in failure

Graph without pretext

A fractured word recalled

If tincture instead of territory

One by one invisible

Taking them back

Agrapha

Giving up isn't giving in, but a different kind of poverty
and if we didn't mention them all in order, it wasn't our fault:
our strength gave out before the daylight tapered,
schedules were strict, the weddings obliged to go forward

even with strangers involved, and sisters and mothers of strangers,
playing Russian roulette with five bullets coughed into the chamber
and swallow the razor and other old parlor games,
keeping appointments with overcoats and nautical charts of the crime

while bosses kept telling lies about factory bylaws, saying
Don't be afraid, I have called you by name, you are mine
and almost believing it, survivors peddling insomnia's cure,
calculating which bridges to burn, which heretics, which beds:

a package that never arrived from a mispronounced province
or a lightswitch left on overnight at the back of the hall,
rehearsing the wreckage of telegrams, padlocks, and skeleton keys
and storms on the coast with other betrayers to please.

Of Which Brought to Bear

By moving inside each other as less

A calm before the storm than storm itself

Wherein elastic premises emerged

From a summer that leaned to the left

Names at a discord, forfeiting visit

Shards of silver that darken, resolve

One climate masquerading as another

Enshadowed by what was likewise in shadow

Extrinsic until unravel until rewoven

Sworn and severe, not her breath alone

Breaketh for the longing it hath unto

The rapt, the fugitive candors

Late misguided extravagant

Say there was not malice in that avail

From North Port

Honing a minor seventh chord on its shear,
mainsail and jib both inhaling,

we're leaning away from ourselves,
tracing water at six and a quarter knots.

Lubber needle twitches,
finding 10° off North

and dusk is spinning the sparfly
counterclockwise.

The half-thawed coast
unzipping to tree line and garbage,

the keel keeps slipping by slanted docks
and propane channel lights.

Fishbox mills and icehouses wait
while we pray toward the darker course,

holding our breath all the way into harbor.

Part Two

Mise en scène

*What you have come to is nothing known
to the senses: not a blazing fire, or a gloom
turning to total darkness, or a storm; or
trumpeting thunder or the great voice
speaking which made everyone who heard
it beg that no more should be said to them.*

HEBREWS 12:18—19

i.
Corona

The sky moves one way and the ground goes the other. Between aurora bo-
realis and the methane-bleached clump of grass at the gulch's rim, there has
always been this window, knotted with ligaments scoring the forest to cross-
hatch. You cannot trace it, it will not offer its name. Fog cresting in off the
lake, the mailbox etched with snow at the edge of the orchard, a russet fox
nubbing the privet, skullcap bulbs in the hillside: it's out behind the house,
parting the shadows webbed between the tar barrels. Already it is slipping
into the tissue of the next moment, where it will not be born or recalled.
Turn back to the fire in the ditch and the boneless tracks. Walk over crab
apple stubble and ice-lathered twigs: November will follow another sound.

ii.
Kinzua

To walk out here is to assume a cartographer's twitch: charting flooded river swills below the dam, noting undulations in the bean field, marking the angle of birches and their ratio to barren space, measuring the rail-line through overgrown cotoneaster. The hail is a god eroding into the past; the runoff accretes into knuckles and broken incisors. Keep going in any direction: darkness is a matrix of pain and belief in the cataract's law. You have graphed the forensics of deer spines and their deterioration. It's not that you can hold the bone and marrow together: it's that you will not allow the sinews to be torn apart.

iii.
Cantus

What it offers and what it withholds are the same: the refined inheritance of neglected towns. Steel girders frame the welding shop to an exoskeleton around the rest of the day. Wires coiled in nooses and spliced intestines, forklifts droning an oratorio to the gravel, sintered metal surging on pulleys and gears: this is the sound of bones on their way through the aircage. The hillside is piled in a scaffold of tires, iconography of an orange and indigo lapse. Don't bother counting what changes more slowly than you do. Pick up what's dropped, index the rate of collapse. Oil rig, gasworks, glass plant, paper mill: listed, and turned away from, and a light going on in the neighborhood, where nobody does anything and everyone complains that nothing gets done.

iv.
Diacritics

Out past the granite quarry, a train hurries somewhere else, its click and clack and coal combustion bringing dawn to the garden. The grammar of everything moving: fricatives of a woodpecker shaving an oak to less and less, sibilants of bumblebees in their cargo-runs from one rhododendron to another. There's little to do these days but sit in a lawn chair and measure how your shadow eats itself slowly and spits it back out. Everywhere the morning tearing up into daybreak through bald roots, the scribble of crossed wires beneath the fertile arras. For every inch of dirt here, there is a country accounted for over those green-ruffled peaks, unconjugated and tenseless. A murmur under the tilted redbird feeder, a scurry and nip in the pachysandra, leg vein and leaf vein, worm glaze and wasp shell, calico blight and bruises smudging the pear, frost and unfreezing, the water and where it goes, dark knot of rain unknotting: ask to be that diver falling haĉek into this wave.

v.
Praxis

Your face is the afterimage of a lost trajectory. The steps descending lead back up behind you: what's down here has receded into the salt of ocean drone, and beneath the narcotic northern lights, a calculus of glaciers efface an unspoken helix. There are codes you know nothing about, but of which you are no less a part. Midnight is a gesture in excavation, an exercise in unstringing the constellations. But fissures still keep the archaeology of live and die: a frightened gull and the arrow that intercepts.

vi.
Conewango

Submerged now in the tadpole slaver and creosote thaw of spring, rotting in strands and cased in rivulets like bronchial tubes, it's not worth finding out where this bridge might lead. It was laid makeshift out of railroad ties by boys playing guns or the old men they became, foraging golf balls. The dampened soot of a pheasant hunter's campfire and sow bugs aerating stagnant earth urge you to stay on this side, the owner is away and you don't belong here. Everything leans in as if passing a rumor: what the charcoal eye of the crayfish says to the stone, what mushrooms shelving the pine stump say to the thrush, is bound to have changed by the time it reaches a clearing.

vii.
Covenant

Follow that noise which beckons you toward the border: the road through the forest passes an arsenal of gutted gasoline pumps and a trailer park sunk in the field like a cellar. Children administer last rites to a strangled jay and guard the vacant parking lot, holding pattern to the next world. Take your spark plugs, pistons and bile to the landfill: the work in this valley is weather and death, with never an extra hour. And all the while the rain will not let up, chamfering the fevered mud and scrawling hieroglyphs. The ground swells to talc and tallow, and flooding delays the night, as though water were keeping the light from leaving too soon.

viii.
Witness

Untapped and undisturbed, the maple trees stiff in a dark Allegheny wind. Flush of the dam in the distance, night clouds hurrying by. The moss on every stone and root slick with day end, the scrawny cry of crows making their way elsewhere. A tin-roof cabin at the foot of the gully, smoke winding up from its slanted chimney, welding coming unstuck, the lights on inside, someone there and pretending not to be.

ix.
Incognito

It won't be long now: ice like anvils crowding the eavespouts and gutters, roof hammered into corrugation. The day is darker sooner, night's gossamer performing its service, the front yard anesthetized, backyard already in coma. There are few alternatives but to sweat among the rattling hemlocks and survey the beetles in their glassy stasis. Begin your lament for the disappearing sun strophes, know that what is missing is always here. Renounce the footworn ladder rung and the bent nail: the sonar will find you leaning into the crimson of a near coast, or gone under, or stranded on a chiseled peak, clinging to the serif of an unknown letter.

x.
Penumbra

Discipline, to reduce the world to integument: charred jawbones among peat smoke and fir cinders, skin on the estuary pleated and braided with bubbles, the arrogance of pond rushes frozen to angled follicles, and forgotten. Coiled in their nest like wrinkled ghosts, newborn mice open to hunger and the stringent hawk. What the weather vane does will not alter the weather, iron flecking off in the pipes and fire starting blue in the hayloft. Seek to unravel impatience and align yourself to meanwhile: the stigmata trail stops at the salt box, backdraft emerges cauterized through bladed branches. Only a sewer line away, the cliffs hang slashed to a sickle swipe, and the painted light of a crude star years ago.

xi.
Doxologia

What came before was something given up, an exchange of one for the other, and the cemeteries are perforated with mines. What will come after is marked by the crows that conduct it. Two points brace the interim ellipse: you, and your voice displaced a cenotaph away. You have come here to pay attention to the north flossed through a subzero flue, to repeat the grief corolla. An orchestra pierces the snowflux and sulfur, that place where all the lost things go for too long. Listen: the air has been missing for months, and already the light is struggling in the caesurae of a further note, dispatches from the god who prays to us.

xii.
Ephphatha

Going to bed late and waking up early: sun is rouging the west dune escarp-
ment, and soon it will have trawled the receding coast, past the splintered
fishing pier into tomorrow. The sepals are stencilled with saltwater froth,
concrete blocks a grille for lichen and cinders. Listening knows how the nega-
tive aperture works, and what it reveals in the nets. The northeastern gales
are soughing their plea through the lighthouse, waves are stammering apoc-
rypha and graffiti. Solder yourself to the hyphen in midnight and morning:
nightfall will leave you sitting alone on the docks, nodding to the metro-
nome of buoys and sieved through the fog: the letter that came with the
signature missing, you waited for that for weeks.

xiii.
Eidolon

Weight is the syntax of filling empty spaces: scalpels and expired tissue fall, but fire rises to fever and sere. Write your unanswered prescriptions ahead to the weather, increase the dosage, trace diminuendo into line. Stop walking and the ward will move backward, until out of the order of lazars and lesions, some caustic Asclepius pretending to pass through the white cell walls of April, March, *februare:* to expel from a house those shadows the dead have diseased.

xiv.
Sanctus

Daylight savings, and all the art schools are closed. Somewhere in the wind corridor the pianos are beginning, and rain suggests staccato out on the beaches. Tell yourself that suffering is what was born on the seventh day, that silence only enters when the motions of the body fall away. The clouds are no good to you now: exit the station while morning dismantles its promise. Conduct yourself by the hidden heuristics of alpha and endgame, ask for forgiveness when distance compels you to travel. And evening arrives ahead of the tide, as if an angel were dragging behind her the winter of where she had come from, and why.

xv.
Anachoresis

It's a question of what you will tell them, and who you will tell them has sent you, writing fire and watching the syllables burn. The light, always eight minutes old, has been hung out to dry: plead for the pardon that will not be granted tonight, nor any night. The dusk curve does not have to limit your shadow's erasure: if you keep moving west, and quickly enough, the ice floe will thaw, the darkness will never catch up.

xvi.
Nocturne

There's a restlessness back in the elm grove tonight, tugging at the whitened seams of your voice. This is familiar weather: starched moon strung in the capillary branches, a rustle before the squall and the sky making room. The streets are empty, the air is straitening the rooftops to finepoint. One corner is always at the cost of another, the blackened hedge or messages squibbed on the lake. Keep your eye on the ridgeline, never lose sight of winter's hem. This is how you'll like to remember yourself: standing slightly apart and moving away, knowing in that last tawny rush of the leaves: what goes out there, it never comes back.

Part Three

Postcard

—so this is into extremity poised

and that was staying more or less the same:

the difference was frost on the property wire,

to say nothing of the trains I'd heard before

and listen, the girl saying no stopped to tell me,

how everything keeps going by:

burnt grass is cracking again in the wind,

the orchard renouncing its name and its pallor

for someone to copy on wet sand or bone

and leave for the others to read

when the weather gets better:

I don't know if I told you or not

but what I found that day in the half-light

     out where the apples were done for the year

has given no end to the road twisting down

     from the house, and I've spent a good part

of mornings just watching for day:

     it's still strange to me that the ocean returns,

that lungs will not hold less than what they need:

     but there was fire, in a clearing

under a razorblue sky before dusk

     and I almost couldn't believe that ingathered air:

as if I'd forgotten my hunger, the clearing,

     smoke and the smell of the smoke

Parallax

What it meant when a wave broke in rings
or went about its business finding the end
we couldn't know: there were openings

in the wrinkled forecast of last year's corduroy islands
and other arrivals and other half hours to visit:
sunspots second-guessing the distance to autumn,

that house standing next to its third coat of paint
or a diver about to shiver along his last cliff,
while someone you've overheard but never met

is already asking, as if she'd forgiven herself,
and taking your hand to find traces or reasons
undressing out there in the dark: how a wave knows itself

from another, and if you've seen countries
where twilight and morning don't work, and even trade places.

Slipknot 4

When that which once gave is now given

To the edge of the box

Stunned but intact

To interfere to adjust to excise

And cannot follow cannot access

Counterfeit and disencounter

Promise of dusk

Unhoused lens

Only once, if that

Lessons in Chiaroscuro

I

You once said that while love is lever
to movement and where its trajectory
ends, it never immerses in motion:

so, at least at the edge of today,
the sun extracted a silhouette from every
mailbox and telephone pole, projecting

their possibility into the wind
without assuming ulterior of its own.
Veined by white a week old, junipers

kept on repeating themselves, composed
in wood and its negative trace, a blurring
of branches once-removed and not angled

against imitation or symmetry.
And in the space being occupied
by a pine at the side of the valentine run,

it was a fact that no other object
could be there, though I stood as close
as sap and shagged bark would allow,

trying to read the direction from needles,
to unfix their axis, replace it with air,
hardly aware that I knew less than nothing,

which is what I know now.

II

If facing north means writing against the sun,
given the scripted attitudes and revisions
I posit and soon feel impoverished by

and cannot inhabit or wander around in
even as a guest; and if this studied violence
is less and less accompaniment

to a grandeur seeking a tone of completion,
as day comes to rest, for an instant, on a line
towing night, before sinking through, but is only

correction of local error, saving an hour,
not more, when the season requires:
then preludes, the moment they happen

are epilogue, the greenhouse and its solemn
surroundings withdraw, and snow, like everything
premised on sequence, here in the fireman's park,

is continuous in its diminishment
while falling. Daylight, which does not arrive
any longer, is a souvenir of ordinary persistence

that didn't endure, a choreography's end,
assuming a dancer; and what's not written
is already, even now, before spring has begun,

a history of winter.

III

Then it must be a form of elegance, a privacy
not textured with subordinate coloration,
properties graphed by fences and painted trees

or peripheries which accompany other proposals
defined by participation in an ecology
of the exterior: to stand alone

not violating the borders of the body,
and to watch, as a maestro might study
the self-containing apparatus he motions

and then steps away from:
the sun and its mercurial probability
going up, to level above an arctic isolation

as a fixture, before assembling its hesitancies
into particular light, a single notation,
and reverting to the ridge from which it started.

In that place, comprehending each time zone
at once and casting a shadow in none,
like one *for whom the world has turned*

to several speeds of glass, you would be the sum
of your expansions, a telephoto reduction
in restraint, and part of the hoisted overture

which you impart. Tipped on its axis, the solar
circuit would not make direction diverse,
and you, arrayed to that linear curve,

would fit inside the half-degree dividing Polaris
from polar. Not to involve a bowed vector
of progress, not to think east from ideas of west,

but a bending to straightness, like ice
being thawed, concave or convex without protest
or need: so that posture, resisting speed,

might pose as prayer.

Slipknot 5

Invite in trip wire trained on a shard

Infidelity halved at the rail

Waiting for that which was sent to its owner

Neither forsworn nor forgiven

Invite glycerin invite the blue rasp

Let what was untimely interred be exhumed

Hear me forward and backward

Wherein and whereupon

As quincunx or curative as eschar

The torn thing tearing further

Velocity among the Ruins of Angel Republic

I

In that gesture toward signing the stages to fullness,
even if nothing went without saying, or everything stayed
despite what's been said, distance would have to be structured with all the rest.

Turning around would be figured in too, since what was back there
could only distract, or weaken the will to keep rowing away
from rooftops and towers with ladders propped up,

the customs house and its officer, blind, standing in sunlight
waving good-bye, as if another had already paid for my ticket.
A school had been built on the island from hammered-out hulls,

fallout shelters lit by old lanterns, a hospital covered in palm fronds and snow,
a bunkhouse where boys dreamed of walking on tightrope to morning.
There were uniforms folded on fishline with no one to fill them

and statues too far from the shore for their shadows to reach.
It meant taking whatever heals, or offers a lesser regret for a greater
after loss, being lost, or finding oneself alone and still in love,

framed by a picture that never got painted of parting the water
to measure both sides, here where the trees and the hanged men below
are waiting with me for the branches to break.

II

The weather bureau, he told me, has just announced calm on the coastlines
under a constant assembly of clouds, and whether sirocco evasions
have been handed down or sent up from the colonies,

they're certain to pass one another in transit, since tariffs are higher
after the war, and people ignoring the news from that country have never
exercised themselves with death or prayer. But at the interior

a city resists the dueling hydraulics of maskchange and moonshine
    frequencies
and the stars in that town flicker like a pierrot drinking honeybees
from a teacup, while leaves keep brimming silver along the sand. It's years,

he said, since the acrobats left, and sundials relinquished ownership of air
to a murder of crows, but the monument shading the courtyard is there,
near sulfur lamps staining pink the settings of cirrus. And whenever

the prologues to night are enacted, the dimming sun and its grace note gloss
on the bay—listen, you'll hear your self-portrait unveiling, an angelus
rising out of indifference, to haunt you with a blueprint of such vacancies

by which we visit ourselves. Those who live here say little of being forgiven
while sculling the waves, but passing into where sirens don't answer,
no longer remember which came before, the punishment or the pain.

III

So that, in a further vicinity, under another arcature, I might be counted
among them, the sceneries sculpted their marble seductions in luminous
    balance,
piano-wire drizzle, a filigree archive to puzzle whomever would watch it

from a balcony, or the gardener's doorstep, sampan docks where conclusions
awaited departure, and motioned for clearance. Matchflare and torpor, without
interruption, were part of the furniture, nuanced in polish, and instruments

glinting long after the surgeons had gone. Almanacs and atlases made no
    mention
of lesser solitudes, the survey outlining airdrome and hangar, acres once flushed
by acetylene flares, but what I pulled up there, in galvanized strips, kept
    leading

toward an accumulation of dusk, a gutted lighthouse from which I could see
prerogatives placed in an order no breath could disturb. The gulf's exertions
gave way to a silence, and raindrops, like questions, beaded the huts to conduct

a woman arranged on a parasol bridge, an aspect of twilight, a choir in herself,
tapping frozen glasses with a spoon, as embers, a chromatic scale,
processions of cartwheeling lights and what else could be staged: tinted water

poised in mid-falling on landscapes still steaming in darkness, a study in form,
geographies pitched at the vanishing point of appearance concealing desire:
space for a leaning, a pivot of air, for where we would stand in that storm.

From the Book of Divine Consolation

as if to escape were part of what it meant to strip to nothing

§
water studying moss on a cliff, to rewrite the slant in carpskin and pipeline,
bottle glass warped by wind and an overdue rain

if someone skips it across

too great to call over or answer

§
forced by flashlight and echo

§
finished rowing downriver, upwind, evening evening out to summer between

bone is thicker than muscle and blood and sinks to the bottom of water

§
wait, resist, be willing

staying the angle's erosion for two hundred years, untouched except by storms

paused but never stopped working

§
since punished for desiring air

looking and having failed, though he found it himself and called it his own

reminded by another stone or object on its way down

§
might break, but is faithful, and trusts her that much: it follows

Slipknot 6

Nor would it stop at the edge

Dissever in three shades of arouse

Wrest us not asunder or aft

Do not deliver us unto

A cataleptic census

Lifted into uncertain proximities

River rationed every stone

Circumflex minus rictus or sieve

A burnt man carrying wood

Not partway the dead die of thirst

Wreckage if not of reckoning

Water without a face but returning

Imago slipped in contingency

Zero inherit sfumato or warp

Afterward as in raze our resistance

The entering into thereof

Isotopes: For Two Voices

[FIRST VOICE]

Let us concern ourselves. There was a proxy moon, embalmed in the cinderella pond, unlearning iridescence under a stagnant, backward sky. Morning waited for weeks at slipped hinges, and we paused to listen for signs of an emptiness starting. Purposeful accidents followed, wherever we went: you could tell by the damage done to the late evening air, even if what the satellites told us was wrong.

[SECOND VOICE]

Rhetoric was calling a parachutist that tree being drawn across grass, toward an afternoon it sketches and moves itself into, like a speaker walking ahead of her own words spoken. The sun and the man were one in their falling, the first made a shadow of the second possible. We might have been part of that slow composition if rack-and-pinion had not, in the end, accelerated to steel. We would wear nothing but open umbrellas, to focus our eyes where the pilot went down.

[FIRST VOICE]

But to erase and to pray are the same in the mind of the motion, if flying is leaving behind a position once fixed. By which I mean that we too must go: separately, out of ourselves and each other, as a speaker, having spoken, exits her speech. There shall not be further blessing from one to another, for fear of the overhearings which only condemn. We must keep a more urgent appointment, burning this field of the wreck and its record, so the moon, when it gets here, is clean.

Autopsy

the wrapper can also be wrapped in its turn, as though the sun drew its reflected radiance from the moon

§

the planet is spinning like a swollen bladder, leaving a faint aftertrace

estrangement & renewal

§

Pompeii

protection vs. crowds & other bodies

§

my wife leaves papers & stuff around on the table, & I love my wife, but mild flirtations w/the housewife next door as far as the eye can see

§

obsessions w/calcium & cholesterol are an unhappiness that doesn't know its name

not some mannerist parabola

§

someone sick & nauseous, resting on a fire hydrant, & the passengers cool their heels at a small local airport, when the villain unexpectedly emerges, over your shoulder

§

less intermissions than fleeting opportunities to visit the bathroom or throw a sandwich together

§

meanwhile, a nostalgia for nostalgia

gangsters & escaped convicts wearing bowler hats carry umbrellas & will
return to such interpretive possibilities later on

people who did that kind of thing in those days, now busy doing
something else

§

a pill one had to swallow in spite of its sugarcoating

a convenient place to take it out on children, who, archaeologists tell us,
bumped into each other a lot, were frequently confused, had short
attention spans, milled around w/o identifiable purpose

§

a man is trying by phone to persuade a woman to continue

§

dust of empty spaces

under the soldier's left arm

nobody stayed home to mind the store

the airplane finally in the process of landing

§

a rising or a setting sun

Ascension Proviso

Not, not yet, this ever revolving speculum of abeyances and ardor

its facile, its vagrant facade, not narrowing into corridors of lease

fervor fulfils an iris without exhausting engines to further advance

edifice courting luster and lust, arisen along enamor defying ascent

fragrant so the tissue bearing tremors, coaxed by a finger, a tongue

Ascension Proviso

Whose crux it wore aghast without reason, where else traveling led

roulade to linger past augur and singe, runoff the spar over frames

her body did not know the difference, the lengths to which she went

one inside the arraignments of another's standing outside her shape

as among the revisions, luring some crest from the contract it keeps

Ascension Proviso

After convicted in the visible, breaking from as anxiously as before

swerve and cut away, these raptures force the night to stay its pulse

spurn such distance the heaving, the heat, rubbing avast of the skin

water froze out back and dazzled winter where it stuttered, stopped

darkest, she said, appropriate, cold, averse to all but the vagaries of

Ascension Proviso

Caught between incision and fragment, rapport of once and never

split from the sinews that centered each other in contexts nullified

propping the question ajar, storm windows shattered by certainty if

lavish one might learn to call it, except for a parallel, indigent rift

would not have exerted an answer, lashing an almost lover allows

Ascension Proviso

Resistance uttered but no less adhered to, washing what the revenant

coming apart at the seams of her selfhood, not ecstasy but nearly ex-

protocols to intervene, attrition eliding the sheets, the shame, and yet

bereft of the senses that burden, beguile, dare not the lenient weight

dare not restitution of whatever walls once held these halves in place

Slipknot 7

Dark be not dark but some other decision

End there is no end

Pirouette of a staircase unlit

Inured to undertow

Of argument or an exit opposed

Prologue there is no prior

Frozen conjecture the slant in the current

Interpose account and accord

Disclosure of disguise

During which time it unraveled it held

Came to pass in its passing it held

O iron us into exclusion

O what if not this if not naked or knit

Some other destitution or demise

Dark be not dark but some other desire

§

Ampersonata

& day not breaking but already broken

& someone holding another to privilege day

& beauty is for the living, at the perimeter, not the last

& look, so quiet we hear each other think

& a lake that fell off the edge of the eye

& clearing away the rubble, & clearing away the rubble

& days of grace, moments of anguish of course

& I don't understand, I understand

& praise without & do not look back

& call it leaving the lights off, or leaving the lake for another lake

& accommodate the feint & forfeiture, & do not look

& nothing else will trade places again

& not only waving but waving again & except

& what will never be seen, never known at the edge of the eye

& water purling in carets to cover the mirror

& memoirs of air & memoirs of

& eavesdropping on the eyelids of morning

& light & less than light—

       even so, even so

Notes

The epigraph is from *The Trinity* 4.1.2.

Part One

"Astrelegy" is for Ryan Zawacki. The italicized lines paraphrase a James Wright translation of Juan Ramón Jiménez.

The title "Wherefrom the Shadows that Are Forms" is a phrase from Robert Duncan's "Often I Am Permitted To Return To A Meadow."

"Ventriloquy" is for Mark Strand.

The someone in the first line of "Note from Anotherwhere" is Tomaž Šalamun.

"Self-Portrait" is after Aristotle's *De Anima* II.7: "It is that which is colorless which is receptive of color."

"Any Other Eviction, Than the Frequent" takes its cue from Job 7:1: "The life of man is a warfare upon earth."

Agrapha is Greek for "the unwritten places." The italicized line is from Isaiah 43:1.

The eleventh line of "Of Which Brought to Bear" is from Psalms 119:20.

Part Two

"*Mise en scène*" is for Aleš Debeljak.

Kinzua and *Conewango* are Seneca names, the former for a region, the latter for a creek, both in northwestern Pennsylvania.

Ephphatha is the Aramaic phrase which Christ speaks in Mark 7:34 to cure someone of deafness and stammering. It means, "Be opened."

Anachoresis is Greek for "withdrawal" or "displacement."

Part Three

"Parallax" is after Kazimir Malevich's "*Maison rouge,*" and its opening line reprises a question in Virginia Woolf's *To the Lighthouse.*

The italicized phrase in the third of the "Lessons in Chiaroscuro" is adapted from Wallace Stevens's "The Bouquet."

The first part of "Velocity among the Ruins of Angel Republic" is for Benjamin Zawacki and includes a line adapted from Kevin Hart's "The Ship." The second part, after Yannis Ritsos's "The Other City," includes a line adapted from "Veterans' Club" by Brian Henry, to whom it is dedicated.

The title "From the Book of Divine Consolation" is after Meister Eckhart.

"Autopsy" is composed of phrases taken from Fredric Jameson's *Postmodernism, or, the Cultural Logic of Late Capitalism* (Verso, 1991).

§

"Ampersonata" is for Scott Lindsey and *in memoriam* Yulia Zelmanovich (1971–1998).

The Contemporary Poetry Series

EDITED BY PAUL ZIMMER

The Contemporary Poetry Series

EDITED BY BIN RAMKE